Top 10 Fun Pets for Kids 9 – 12: Best Beginner Pet Owner Choices

Fun Pets For Kids Book 2

Jacquelyn Elnor Johnson

www.CrimsonHillBooks.com/best-pets-for-kids

© 2017 Crimson Hill Books/Crimson Hill Products Inc.

All rights reserved. No part of this book may be copied, lent, excerpted or quoted except in very brief passages by a reviewer.

Cataloguing in Publication Data

Jacquelyn Elnor Johnson

Top 10 Fun Pets for Kids 9-12

Description: Crimson Hill Books trade hardcover edition | Nova Scotia, Canada

ISBN 978-1-988650-90-6 (Hardcover)

BISAC: JNF003170 Juvenile Nonfiction: Animals - Pets | JUV002190 Juvenile Fiction: Animals - Pets

THEMA: YNNH - Children's / Teenage general interest: Pets & pet care | YNN - Children's / Teenage general interest: Nature, animals, the natural world | YN - Children's / Teenage: general interest

Record available at https://www.bac-lac.gc.ca/eng/Pages/home.aspx

Cover design, Book design and formatting: Jesse Johnson

Crimson Hill Books
(a division of)
Crimson Hill Products Inc.
Wolfville, Nova Scotia
Canada

This is a black and white pet rabbit. Photo by Rhae courtesy of Pixabay.

For Teachers and Parents

When kids think of pets, they think of fun. Their minds are full of all the fun things they're going to do with their new pet, really soon!

But the first thing adults think of when the pet question comes up is responsibility. This begins with making good decisions. Is the pet they want really the best pet for them? And for your family or classroom?

Parents and teachers want children to get the pet that's:

- safe (for both pet and child),
- easy to care for and keep healthy,
- pleasant to live with and
- a pet they'll continue to enjoy.

To be a best pet for kids, or pet owners of any age, this creature also needs to have fairly straightforward care requirements that children can manage with minimal adult intervention.

Most teachers and many parents also expect a pet to be inexpensive both to buy and to maintain.

Children are focused on all the fun they'll soon be having with their new pet. They're excited that it will live in their room, or their classroom.

Hold your pet securely. They don't want to feel like they could fall but they also don't want to be squished. Photo by Westfale courtesy of Pixabay

Adults want kids to enjoy pets, but they also want kids to gain the life lessons caring for a pet can provide, such as:

- thinking beyond their own needs and taking responsibility,
- kindness to others,
- compassion, especially for those smaller or weaker than yourself,
- respect for all creatures and for our natural world,
- and another important life skill, cleaning up messes without complaining about it.

So what pets are the top 10 fun pets that delight kids while meeting the needs of their teachers and parents?

Here they are. This lively chapter book is written on the fourth-grade reading level for kids 8-12.

In general, these creatures are bred in captivity as pets, widely- available and proven kid-pleasers.

However, you should know that some pets are not legal in some cities, states or provinces. Check local laws or restrictions online, by asking your vet or at a rescue shelter, such as The Humane Society or SPCA. Pet rescues are also where you can find healthy, vet-checked, socialized pets in need of caring homes.

Before adopting a pet, be sure to have a veterinarian lined up. They need to be a vet who's experienced with the specific pet you choose (unless this pet is a fish. Pet store staff are usually knowledgeable about fish ailments and treatments).

This book tells you about each pet, what it's like to have them, basic care and why they'd be a fun pet for young pet owners.

Generally, the pets in this book and all pets aren't suitable for very young children unless you can constantly monitor the safety of both child and pet.

Once you and your child (or class) have chosen the best pet, you'll probably want them to do more reading about this pet's diet, housing and health needs.

This book is designed to be the starting point, introducing children, or any new pet owner, to all the best fun pets there are and what it's like to have them.

We are pet owners, not veterinarians. Nothing included in this book is meant to serve as medical advice. If you suspect your pet is ill, please see your local vet. We accept no liability concerning your pet ownership.

Contents

CHAPTER 1 - FUN PETS FOR KIDS 9

CHAPTER 2 - HAMSTERS 15

CHAPTER 3 - GERBILS 22

CHAPTER 4 - GUINEA PIGS 27

CHAPTER 5 - RATS............................. 32

CHAPTER 6 - RABBITS 38

CHAPTER 7 - CHINCHILLAS 46

CHAPTER 8 - SNAKES........................... 51

CHAPTER 9 - COCKATIELS 58

CHAPTER 10 - KITTENS OR CATS 64

CHAPTER 11 - PUPPIES OR DOGS.............. 69

CHAPTER 12 - HOW TO BRING YOUR NEW PET HOME 76

CHAPTER 13 - WHAT PET WILL YOU GET?... 82

THANK YOU FOR READING! 85

Chapter 1
Fun Pets for Kids

What makes a pet fun? Why do kids and adults enjoy this pet?

What makes a pet easy enough for beginner pet owners? How much work involved?

What is it really like to have a pet?

These questions are answered in this book about the top ten fun pets for kids who are ages 9 to 12.

Things to think about before you choose your pet:

- Do I want a small pet, a medium-sized pet or a larger pet?
- Do I want an indoor pet or one that I can play with outside?
- Do I want a pet that doesn't live for a very long time, or one that will still be alive when I'm a teenager or even longer than that?
- Do I want a pet that can learn to do tricks?
- How much time do I have every day to look after my pet and play with them? Will I still

A girl with her pet rabbit. Photo by Emily True on Pixabay.

clean their cage or take them for walks even when I don't feel like it?

- Who will pay for this pet? Will I use my allowance, or money gifts or get an after-school job to help pay for my pet and everything they need?

How much will a pet cost?

How much it costs to get your pet and everything they need varies, depending on which pet you chose and where you get them.

You can buy most of the pets in this book and their cage or bed and food for $100 or less. But remember, you'll need money every month for everything else your pet needs – food, toys and possibly veterinarian bills if your pet gets sick. A veterinarian is a pet doctor.

Are you ready to be a good pet parent?

Here are some serious questions to ask yourself. Think carefully about your answers.

1. Am I a kind person? Do I understand how to be gentle with pets?
2. How much time will my pet spend in their cage? How much time do I have to play with them?
3. Am I a patient person who won't get angry if my pet makes a mess that I must clean up?
4. Can I make a promise to this pet that I will always give it everything it needs to be healthy and happy?
5. Can I make a promise to myself and my family that I won't let my pet, my family or myself down in this commitment?
6. Am I person who keeps their promises?

What to do if your parents say, "No pets."

Your parents or teachers may decide that getting a pet isn't a good idea for your home or classroom. If so, there are things you can do to possibly change their decision.

Here's what won't work: crying, begging for a pet, pleading, or getting angry.

Here's what to do instead. Think very carefully about all the questions and things to think about asked earlier in this chapter.

Get a notebook and write down your answers.

Read these answers over. Think about them.

Read this book to help you choose the pet that you want that is also a good choice for you and your family or class.

Write what you know about the pet you choose in your notebook. Write about why this pet is a good choice that will fit in with your life and your family.

Organize these notes with your thoughts into a report. Use it to make a presentation to your class or your family.

After you do this, they might still say you can't have the pet you want. If they do, ask why. It could be that they have good reasons for saying, "No pets." Consider what these reasons are.

And leave the pet question, for now. In a year or so, things might have changed. You'll be a bit older and have had more opportunities to show your parents that you're a responsible person who is ready to look after a pet. Then, you can try again with your Pet Presentation.

If they say yes, you'll need to...

Get ready before you bring pet home

To get ready, you need to buy everything your pet will need.

Set up their bed or cage. Then, pet-proof the rooms where they'll be allowed out to play.

Know as much as can about your pet, what they like, what they eat and what health problems they can have before you get your pet.

When you bring your pet home, don't expect them instantly to be a fantastic pet. Remember, they've suddenly left everything they know. They're frightened. Their entire world has changed.

Give them time to get settled before you bring them out to play. Let them gradually get used to you. Never try to reach into their cage and grab them. Wait until they are comfortable coming to you.

If you are kind and patient, they will soon learn to trust that you're taking good care of them. This means never forgetting to give them fresh food and water, never forgetting to clean their tank or cage, and never walking past their tank or cage without some kind words.

Even 'easy' pets have special needs. Some are very afraid of the noise of a vacuum cleaner, or thunder storms, or larger animals. Some hate it when you wake them up suddenly. Some just need time alone to rest sometimes. It's cruel to laugh at their fears. Instead, show them kindness when they're frightened.

Getting to know your pet means respecting them for who they are. They're trusting you to give them everything they need so you can have a long and happy time together with your new BFP (best fun pet).

Remember, there are no 'starter' pets, but there are beginning pet owners. You will need to learn to be a good pet owner, just as the animal in your care is learning to be a good pet.

This hamster has a colorful plastic cage that he can explore. Photo by Etouale on Pixabay.

Chapter 2

Hamsters

Hamsters are a small, curious and lively animal that is one of the easiest pets to have. They're also very inexpensive to buy and to keep. And they like people, once they get to know you.

For these reasons, they are one of the most popular pets for children age 8 and older and beginning pet owners.

All hamsters are pudgy little animals. They have a very short tail, small furry ears, short legs and wide feet. Their silky fur can be black, red, yellow, brown, white, grey, orange or honey-coloured or a colour mix. There are even some that have spots or stripes!

Pet hamsters love tunnels. It can be any kind of tunnel. Maybe this is because tunnels remind them of the underground homes of their wild hamster ancestors.

Today, all pet hamsters are bred to be pets. They were never wild, and neither were their parents or grandparents. But, like all animals, they still

This is a hamster. Photo by Meditations on Pixabay.

remember their survival skills! If you're a small animal, this means knowing how to hide!

Because hamsters enjoy being in small spaces, clear plastic tunnel toys are popular among pet hamster owners. It's fun to watch your hamster making their way up and down the tunnels. Sometimes, they poke their heads out of the openings. They always seem so surprised to see where they are!

You could buy one of these tunnel toys for your pet hamster, but if you do, you'll find that it's difficult to keep it clean.

Here's another idea. Why not make a tunnel maze for your hamster to explore? A maze is like a puzzle, where you must find a path from where you are right now to where you want to go.

Many small pets like mice, gerbils and hamsters enjoy finding their way through a maze, especially if there's a food treat at the end!

You can make your own tunnels and maze with cardboard rolls, milk or juice cartons and shoeboxes. Make ladders with ice cream sticks. Don't build it inside your hamster's cage because that's too small a place.

Instead, you could build your hamster's new playground inside a big box, like the ones new furniture comes in. Or it could be inside a plastic kiddie pool. Or maybe in a small room that you've already hamster-proofed, so there aren't any places they could get hurt or lost.

Hamsters are an easy and safe pet for kids. If they're a bit grumpy, they want to have some time alone in their cage. They mostly sleep during the day, except for early morning or evening, when they like to be active.

If their cage is in your bedroom, you might hear them rustling around and getting a snack through the night. Unless you're already awake, you probably won't hear them.

Be kind to your hamster, and don't ever tease them. They really don't like it when you wake them up suddenly or play roughly. If they squeal, it means they're not happy and they want to bite you.

They hardly ever bite unless they're very stressed or feeling threatened. If they do, you'll find their teeth are sharp!

Hamsters don't see very well, and they can't see in colour. But they have an excellent sense of smell. They use this to find their food. They also have excellent hearing and can hear very high-pitched sounds and ultrasound, something humans can't do.

Can hamsters learn tricks?

Hamsters, like the other small rodent pets, can't do tricks. But they are interesting to watch. They enjoy having people as their friends, once they get to know you.

You don't need to get two hamsters, because they are much happier living alone. If you get two, they will fight.

Hamsters live about 2 to 3 years. Pet hamsters eat hamster pellets. They like their food bowl to always be about ¾ full. They also need a water sippy bottle and a bowl of water in their cage. Give them fresh water every day.

They enjoy fresh vegetables. Feed them shredded kale, collard greens, carrots or sliced zucchini. For treats, give your hamster a slice of apple, banana, melon, seeds, nuts or some raisins or alfalfa hay.

Hamsters' teeth never stop growing. They need to chew to keep their teeth in good condition. Give your hamster chew toys, walnut shells or hard dog biscuits to keep them healthy.

This hamster has a coconut shell to nest in. Photo by Kira Hoffmann on Pixabay.

You might see your pet hamster eat their own poop sometimes. This seems disgusting to people, but many animals do this. It's how they can be sure they get all the nutrients from their food and nothing is wasted.

Their tank or cage is the place where they will eat, rest and sleep. It needs to have a wire mesh top that allows fresh air to get into their tank or cage.

All hamsters are diggers. They like the floor of their cage or tank to have enough bedding that they can dig a sleeping nest. Never use shaved wood or cat litter for bedding. These are dangerous for hamsters. Instead, use shredded paper towels or recycled paper bedding.

When you bring your new pet home, you'll want to sprinkle in a little bit of the bedding from their old habitat to help your new pet feel at home in their new cage.

Hamsters aren't a lazy pet. They like to get some exercise every day. They need a hamster exercise wheel in their cages. When you take them out to play, give them a safe place to run around and explore. This could be inside a kiddie wading pool.

They also enjoy being in a hamster ball on a rug or carpet. You need to watch them when they're in their hamster ball to be sure they're safe. Never let them stay in their hamster ball for more than 20 minutes.

Are you wondering if you should get a male hamster or a female? Males are usually friendlier and more easy-going. But the females are less smelly.

How to clean your pet's cage

Hamsters are a pet that likes to be clean. Just like cats, they will wash themselves with their paws. This can be fun to watch. They also like their food, sleeping place and the corner where they poop to be separate. You'll need to spot-clean their tank or cage every day and do a complete cleaning once a week.

Here's how:

1. Put your pet in a safe place, like in their hamster playground or their hamster ball.
2. Remove the old bedding and throw it away.
3. Wash their tank or cage. Use warm water with some dish detergent mixed in. Use the type of detergent that has no scent. Be sure to get all the corners clean.

4. With fresh soap and water, wash all their toys. If there is still any smell from the soap, mix some vinegar in warm water, wet a paper towel or towel with the vinegar water and wipe down the inside of the tank or cage.
5. Dry everything with an old towel. Be sure it is completely dry.
6. Put in new bedding. It should be about two inches (5 cm) deep.
7. Wash your hands with warm soap and water. Cup your hands, scoop up your hamster and put them back in their clean, dry home.

Where to meet some cool hamsters

A good place to see some of the many types of pet hamsters there are is at a Hamster Show. That's where you'll meet pet hamster breeders and other people who love hamsters. It's a great place to ask questions about having a hamster. It's also where you'll find more unusual pets than you will see in pet stores or at pet rescue shelters.

Hamster Shows are held about once a year in most major cities. You can find dates and other details about one near you with an online search. Put "Hamster Show" and the name of the city in the search bar.

Other pets you might be interested in that are like hamsters are: mice, rats, gerbils, chinchillas and guinea pigs.

Chapter 3
Gerbils

Gerbils look and behave a lot like hamsters because they are a type of hamster. One difference is that they have a long tail that is covered with fur, with a little furry tuft at the end. Their fur can be white, black or gold.

Another is that gerbils are less bitey than hamsters. They have almost no smell, unless you forget to clean their cage for too long!

But just like hamsters they like to dig, they love having toys and they need an exercise wheel in their tank or cage. Make sure their exercise wheel is the type that has a floor and no open bars, because they could easily get their tails caught in the wheel and be injured!

Kids love this pet because they are so friendly. Gerbils are a pocket pet that love to ride around with you, in your sleeve or pocket and do whatever you're doing.

Give them gerbil pellets and, for treats, they like raw oatmeal, peanut butter, popcorn, leafy green

CHAPTER 3 - GERBILS

This is a black gerbil. Photo by Meditations on Pixabay.

vegetables, apple slices and twigs or dog biscuits to chew on. As a special treat, give them sunflower seeds, pine nuts or peanuts.

Gerbils are usually a bit bigger than hamsters, growing to about 6 to 12 inches (150 to 300 mm) long when they're adults.

Don't give your gerbil a plastic tunnel system that is meant for a hamster. It might not be big enough for them and they will chew it. When they do, the plastic could make them sick. It's better not to have any plastic dishes or toys in their tank.

This tank needs to be bigger than one for a pet hamster. Hamsters can live comfortably in a 5 gallon (19 litre) tank, but gerbils need at least a 10 (38 litre) gallon tank. For gerbils, a larger home is always better.

They also need a deep layer of shredded paper towel bedding on the floor and a mesh lid on their tank. You can also use grass hay for bedding. Be careful about the gerbil bedding found in pet stores. It has strands that can get tangled in their feet and hurt them.

Wire cages aren't a good idea because gerbils will chew on the wire and can injure their noses and teeth. Don't choose a plastic cage. They'll soon chew it to pieces!

The cage also needs a sippy bottle of water and a bowl of water in a ceramic bowl. It needs to be heavy enough that your pet can't tip it over.

Give them a nest box for sleeping. A ceramic bowl or flower pot works well for this. Here are some other things to put in their tank or cage or their gerbil playground:

- Things to climb on, like thick pieces of wood, rocks, ladders, ramps and platforms
- Toys that are safe to chew and rodent pet chew sticks
- Paper tubes, like the ones that come with toilet paper
- Soft things for nesting, like shredded paper towel, old socks or scraps of fabric

Clean your gerbil's home with daily spot-cleaning and a total wash every week or so. Follow the same instructions as for a hamster's tank or cage (this is in Chapter 2).

Some pet owners think that they should blow air in a pet gerbil's face to train them not to bite, but this isn't true. Gerbils don't bite unless they're frightened. Blowing in their face can cause a gerbil to have a seizure, which can be mild or serious. Sometimes, a major seizure can kill them.

Losing their tails!

Another odd thing that can happen to a gerbil is losing part or all of their tail. This happens when their tail is injured. First, their tail will lose its fur. Then the tail falls off. Their tail stump usually heals, but they can't grow a new tail.

Gerbils usually live as long as hamsters do; about two or three years. The oldest known pet gerbil lived to be eight years old.

Gerbils get super excited when you let them have a sand bath!

If you decide a gerbil is the right pet for you, get two males or two females. It's best if these two are from the same litter and are at least 5 weeks old, which is old enough to leave their mother.

Gerbils are very sociable and are unhappy living alone.

Cute things pet gerbils can do

Like pet hamsters, gerbils are a little pet that's cute all the time. But then, they'll do something adorable that makes you like them even more!

One of the cute things gerbils can do is stand up on their hind legs, like squirrels.

These little gerbils are just 3 weeks old. Photo by Asatira courtesy of Pixabay.

Gerbils are very curious. They're always exploring.

Two gerbils that live together say, "Hello" by kissing! One will run up to the other and touch noses or their mouths.

Chapter 4
Guinea Pigs

If you want a pet that gets excited when they hear the fridge door open and can't wait for you to come and feed them, you want a cat, dog or guinea pig!

Guineas squeal with excitement when they think it's time to eat!

Guinea pigs are also called cavies. They don't look or act anything like pigs. They look more like a walking dust mop, with a round body, short legs and glossy hair that can be short or long.

The reason they got their name is that they 'talk,' a lot! They can oink and snort like a pig, honk like a goose, whistle like a cockatiel and purr like a cat!

Guinea pigs are like rabbits, but smaller. But unlike pet rabbits, they won't follow you around or come when you call them. They can't learn how to use a litter box.

Besides being cute, cavies can be very friendly and affectionate once they get to know you. And they're one of the easiest pets to care for, making them a popular first pet and a good pet for kids.

This is a mother guinea pig and 2 of her pups. Photo by May Orel via Pixabay.

They don't like to live alone, so if you decide this is the right pet for you, you should get two. It's best if you get two sisters, or two brothers. If you get a male and a female, or two cavies that don't already know each other, they could fight.

Where NOT to put your pet's cage

Rodent pets like gerbils, hamsters, guinea pigs, chinchillas and rabbits need to live indoors in a large cage with a solid floor. The cage can't be in any of these places:

- Outside or anywhere it can get too cold or too hot for your pet.

This variety of guinea pig is long haired. Photo by Lino9999 via pixabay.

- In the garage. Fumes from the car or other things your family keeps out there, like gasoline (petrol) for a lawnmower could kill your pet. Like people, they need fresh air.
- In a drafty place
- In direct sunlight. It gets too hot for your pet.
- Where your pet won't see you. They want to be part of everyday family activities.
- Where their cage could get knocked over.

The best place for a pet's cage is in the living room, a bedroom or a wide-enough hallway.

A cage that's right for a pet chinchilla would also be right for your cavies (see Chapter 7) except it won't need a lid. Cavies aren't climbers and they can't jump very far.

They need a sippy water bottle, a food dish, wood chews and a hiding place to rest and sleep.

Don't give them an exercise wheel. It can hurt their backs and feet.

Shredded paper makes a good cage bedding. Spot clean every day. The cage needs a complete cleaning once a week.

If you have a long-haired pet, they'll need a daily brushing. Short-haired cavies need brushing too, just not as often.

All cavies need their toenails clipped. Ask your veterinarian to show you how to do this safely the first time you take your pet for a check-up. They don't like baths, so only bath your pet if they get into something sticky or dirty.

Cavies love some outdoor playtime in sunny weather. Get a puppy enclosure, so they can nibble on fresh grass, but stay safe.

They need to come out to play on the floor every day for at least a couple of hours. They want to run around and explore. They also want some toys and tunnels in their playground.

When they're in their cage, give them plenty of toys to play with. They love cardboard boxes, soft toys and pieces of paper towel or fabric. You could have fun making them toys out of cereal boxes, paper bags, folders and other things you already have around the house.

Guineas must have hay and fresh vegetables every day. Just like people, their bodies can't make the Vitamin C they need, so they must get it from vegetables. They need 1 cup (250 ml) a day of salad made from any of these: leafy greens, celery, carrots or pea pods. They can have apple slices for treats.

Lawn grass is also good for them, just as long as no chemical weed killer, pest killer or fertilizer has been put on your lawn. These are poisons for pets.

If you feed your adult cavy pellets, they should be plain timothy pellets with no seeds. Baby cavies and pregnant females need to eat alfalfa hay.

Never give your cavy these foods: rocket salad, red leaves, cauliflower, beet greens, radishes or potatoes. Any of these could make them sick!

Cavies are happy pets when you never pass their cage without stopping for a little visit. Talk to them, carry them around your house, and treat them like a furry family member. They want plenty of time with their BPF – their best people friend!

Chapter 5
Rats

Think of a pet that is small, smart enough to understand words and do some tricks, can learn to use a litter box, is happy to go anywhere with you, has soft fur and has a friendly personality.

Do you have a picture of this pet in your mind?

If so, you might be thinking of a small dog. But would you be surprised to find out there's another pet, even smaller, that can do and be all these things?

This little fun pet is the rat. Pet rats are very clean, relatively easy to care for and, once they know you, enjoy being held and cuddled.

These playful pets come in many colours, coat types and sizes. Some fancy rats even have big ears or no hair or no tail.

One reason they aren't more popular is that some people have odd ideas about pet rats. This is because their cousins, the wild rats, are an animal that has spread dangerous diseases in past centuries. Though we now know how to prevent and cure these terrible diseases, people still fear wild rats.

CHAPTER 5 - RATS

Two pet rats. Photo by Missie26870 via Pixabay.

All pet rats are born from pet rat parents. They are sweet-natured creatures who don't deserve the bad reputation wild rats have. And remember, long ago the wild rats didn't plan to get ill and make humans sick. It happened because people stored their food in barns. Rats thought this was a free supply of lots of delicious food and moved into the barns. Illnesses spread because people and animals lived close to each other.

Modern pet rats are fairly easy to keep healthy. Like their rodent relatives who are hamsters, gerbils and mice, pet rats usually live for two or three years.

Rats are the most intelligent of these small pocket pets. They love to explore and learn new things! You could have fun making them a rat castle to explore, with ladders and ramps, doors and windows. If you make your rat fun house out of cardboard boxes or wood, your pet will chew on it. But that just means you get to make them a new rat play house.

Some pet rat owners buy a clicker, like the ones used to teach tricks to dogs. You click the clicker when your pet does something you want them to do. They think hearing the clicks is a reward, like getting a treat. Using a clicker, you can teach smart pets, like dogs and rats, how to do all sorts of funny and crazy things, like:

- Shake a paw
- Come when you call their name
- Jump over an object
- Ride on a toy skateboard

Training time should be short, just 5 minutes. Stop if your pet seems to be tired of the game and try again later. Your pet will have more fun this way, and so will you!

Some rats like having an exercise wheel. It needs to be a large one, with a solid floor, to be safe for your pet.

All rats like puzzles and toys. You could look at a pet store for toys designed for another intelligent pet, parrots. Rats love parrot toys!

Rats with Jobs!

Many intelligent animals do jobs for people. But not many people know that one of the types of animals people use to do some important jobs are rats!

They can help rewire buildings when spaces are too tight for people to get to, act as messengers or carry a critter camera to make TV programs about animals.

Pet Rat Care

Your pet rat could live in an aquarium tank, but a wire cage with a solid floor is better. Be sure to choose one with a large door so it's easy to get your pet out each day for playtime and exercise. A cage that's meant for a pet ferret or guinea pig is the right size for a pet rat.

Rats are intelligent. They can climb. They love to explore. This means they'll try to get out of their cage or tank to have a look around unless you have a top on your rat's tank or cage.

If you choose a tank rather than a cage, it can get smelly in just a couple of days. With both types of homes for your pet, you'll need to spot clean to get rid of wet spots and poop every day. A glass tank will need a complete cleaning every three days. Because a cage home lets in more air, it doesn't get smelly as quickly. You'll need to clean it once a week.

Another good thing about a cage home for your pet rat is they love to have a fleece hammock for relaxing. These are made to hang from the metal sides of a cage. You will need to get two, because pet hammocks need to be washed once or twice a week.

Your rat will also need chew toys to keep his teeth healthy. Chew toys for parrots or hard dog biscuits and dog chew toys will also be good for your pet rat.

Rats need lots of fresh water. A sippy bottle on the side of their cage works, but you'll need to keep buying new ones if your pet chews on the plastic part. You could also put water in a porcelain bowl in their cage. Make sure it is heavy enough that your pet won't tip it over.

Feed your pet small rodent pellets and grains mix. For treats, give them any of these:

- A piece of fresh fruit
- Raw or cooked vegetables or vegetable peels
- Bits of leftover cooked meat
- Breakfast cereal, the kind without sugar added like plain oatmeal or granola
- Trail mix
- Yogurt
- Hummus
- Cheese

If it's a healthy snack for people, it's a healthy snack for your pet rat. So never give them candy, chocolate or salty snacks like chips or salted nuts.

Rats love peanut butter, but it is so thick that they can easily choke on it. If you want to give your rat a PB treat, mix it with melted butter or vegetable oil so it's easier for them to swallow.

Rats are a very clean animal. Just like cats, they like to wash themselves. But if they get into something sticky, they might need a gentle bath. Use baby shampoo, warm water and a soft cloth. Your rat won't enjoy this, so make her bath as quick as possible, dry her completely with another soft cloth and give her a treat when you're done.

You always need to be careful about what bedding you choose for your pet. Never use bedding made from wood because it will make your pet sick. Instead, use a paper litter or shredded paper, paper towel or corncob litter. Never use clumping litter because sometimes your pet could accidently swallow some of it and it will kill them.

People who have rat pets say they are even friendlier than other rodent pets like guinea pigs, rabbits, gerbils and hamsters. But if you decide a rat is the pet for you and your family, they recommend you get two boys or two girls. Rats are used to living in families and are unhappy being an 'only' rat in a people family.

Also, if they have a cage-mate, plenty of food, water and toys, they can be fine on their own for a few days.

Another good thing about choosing a rat as your pet is that they don't cost very much to get or to keep.

What do you call more than one rat?

What do you call it when you have more than one of the same animal as a pet? In English, we have names for groups of animals. So, if you have more than one cat, you have a clowder of cats.

Do you have two or more hamsters? They're called a horde of hamsters.

And what is the group name for rats? Can you guess? It's a mischief of rats!

Find more pet animal group names at the end of this book!

Chapter 6
Rabbits

Have you ever seen someone walking their pet rabbit on a leash at the park? Maybe you thought this looks a bit odd, but some rabbits love to be taken for walks!

And that's not the only surprising thing a pet rabbit can do. They can learn their name and come when you call them. They can also learn to use a litter box, as many cats (and some dogs) can do.

Also, like dogs, pet rabbits want lots of attention and time with their owners. Pet rabbits need to get out of their cage to play and be with you for at least 3 hours every day. Some rabbits want to be out all the time, only going back to their cage to rest or sleep.

Like cats and dogs, rabbits have lots of personality. They can be very affectionate pets who follow you around like a puppy! Once they get to know and trust you, they might hop into your lap for a cuddle.

CHAPTER 6 - RABBITS

This tiny pet rabbit is just a baby. Photo by Incygneia via Pixabay.

There's a lot of variety in the rabbit world. Pet rabbits can have short or long fur that's white, brown, black, honey-golden, gray or a mix of these colours.

Most rabbits have upright ears, but a few have long floppy ears. They can be as small as a guinea pig, up to as large as medium-sized dog.

Just some of the things to like about rabbits as pets are they like to be clean, they are quiet most of the time and they're fun to watch as they hop around, exploring everywhere.

You'll have fun learning bunny body language and what all the sounds they can make mean.

- Clicking their teeth means they're happy, they feel safe and content and they trust you.

- Some rabbits snort when they want attention. Others do this when they're not happy, or when they have a cold. If they snort and have stuff coming out of their nose, they need to see the vet.
- Rabbits whimper when they're afraid or in pain.
- They squeal when they are seriously in pain or afraid. If they do this when you pick them up, the way you are holding them is hurting or they don't trust you yet. Give them time to get to know you.
- When they grind their teeth, they are sick, in pain or very anxious.
- Grunting is another thing rabbits do when they are not happy or they're afraid.
- If your rabbit starts screaming, they're very seriously in pain and could be injured. Rabbits have a delicate skeleton and easily get broken bones. A rabbit that is screaming needs to see the veterinarian right away!
- When they lick you, they are showing that they trust you and like you very much.
- If your bunny flops down in front of you or sits on your lap and lets you cuddle him, it means he is happy and trusts you.
- If she nudges you with her nose, your pet wants you to pet her.

You'll need an indoor bunny cage, bunny condo, rabbit hutch or puppy pen for your pet. Set it up in a place that's away from drafts, direct sunlight and is where they can see family life, but aren't in a noisy place.

These are dwarf pet rabbits. The one on the left is an albino. Photo by Aiedail09 courtesy of Pixabay.

The cage or condo needs to be big enough that your pet can hop around and has separate places to eat, play, rest or sleep and corners away from all these for their rabbit toilet.

Rabbits need to drink a lot of water to stay healthy. A sippy bottle that would work for other pets just isn't enough for your rabbit. Give them a soup bowl or large dog bowl of cool, fresh water and refill it at least once a day.

Their hutch or pen also needs a hay feeder and ceramic or china food bowls that are big enough that your rabbit can't tip them over.

Rabbits get bored when they don't have plenty of toys. You'll see different types of rabbit toys at pet stores, or you can have fun making rabbit toys out of old socks and pieces of fabric.

Rabbits also enjoy a cardboard castle. They'll add more doors and windows and have lots of fun destroying the castle. Then, just give them another one.

Housetraining Your Bunny

Housetraining means teaching your pet where to go so it doesn't pee and poop everywhere. Like kittens, it's very easy to housetrain a pet rabbit. Rabbits will naturally use just one corner, or two corners of their cage for a toilet.

If you want to housetrain your rabbit, put a litter box or a shallow plastic box at the corner (or two corners) they've already chosen for their toilet. You can't use cat litter, because it can be a poison for your pet, making them very sick.

Instead, put a thin layer of recycled newspaper pellet litter in the litter box, with some fresh timothy hay, alfalfa hay, grass hay or oat hay on top for an adult bunny. Baby rabbits should get alfalfa hay only. You do this because rabbits like to munch on hay when they're on their toilet.

You'll need to clean your rabbit's litter box or litter boxes every few days.

How to Bunny-proof Your Home

Bunnies will chew on anything they can get to. Before you let them out of their hutch or cage, you'll need to bunny-proof their room. Do this:

- Remove any wood furniture, because they will chew on it.
- Put a metal baby gate in the doorway.

- Remove power cords, or put them inside plastic sleeves or tubing.
- Cover wood baseboards with plastic guards.
- Remove house plants, books and everything else you don't want your rabbit to chew on.

If you have a yard or garden, you might want to set up a puppy pen outside and let your rabbit hop around, enjoying the fresh air and outdoor smells and nibbling on the grass.

If you don't have outside space, you can still take them to the park. Get one of the harness-style leashes made for small cats. These are also ideal for rabbits. Be careful to never pull hard on their leash because they're easily injured.

Rabbits need lots of exercise, either inside or outside in mild weather, but not when it's too hot out. Remember, they always have to wear a fur coat.

Rabbits must have hay to stay healthy. They also need rabbit pellets and fresh vegetables. For treats they can have raw oatmeal, carrots or slices of apple or banana.

How to Plant a Bunny Garden

One of the fun things to do for your pet rabbit is plant a garden of some of their favourite vegetables. This is easy to do, even if you've never had a garden before or only have space for a few plant containers. You can get these containers at garden centres or find them at yard sales. Or use anything that can hold some soil, like a large heavy-duty shopping tote bag, an old car tire or a wooden packing crate.

Be sure your planter has a few drainage holes in the bottom, so your plants don't get waterlogged. If you have a balcony, put your container on a plant saucer. This is like a big plate with sides so when you water your garden, the water doesn't spill on the floor.

Add a few stones to the bottom of your container, then fill it with potting soil mix. Don't use soil you dig up from outside. It will have insects (like fly eggs) in it and could have other things in it you don't want in the house or on your balcony.

Buy packages of lettuce, bok choy (Chinese cabbage), carrots or herb seeds and plant them, following the directions on the seed packets. Water right away and put in a sunny spot, away from wind.

Good herbs for pet rabbits are basil, oregano, mint, parsley and cilantro.

Rabbits can be a wonderful pet, but before you decide this is the right pet for you, here are some things you should know.

When you have a pet rabbit, you will need to have a vet who treats small animals. One time you will need their help is that you'll need to have your pet neutered, if this hasn't already happened when you get them.

Neutered means having an operation that will make them not able to have babies.

Male rabbits, called bucks, are neutered when they're five months old. This makes them a friendlier, more mild-mannered pet and stops them from spraying pee to mark their territory.

CHAPTER 6 - RABBITS

This pet rabbit is playing outside. Photo by Castleguard via Pixabay.

Female rabbits are called does. Does need to be neutered when they're six months old. This helps protect them from ever getting one type of cancer.

If your family sometimes goes away on vacation, you'll need to hire a pet sitter for your rabbit while you're away, if a friend or family member can't do it. This is because pet rabbits become very upset when they go to a new home. Like most pets, they like having a routine and become very attached to their owner.

With good care, pet rabbits live for five to 10 years.

If you can, choose a baby rabbit or get one that is very young. When they get to know, trust and like people and being handled when they're little, rabbits grow up to be cute, soft, friendly and loving pets.

45

Chapter 7
Chinchillas

Would you like a pet that's a bit unusual, but still fun to play with?

Here's a pet that's just a bit bigger than a wild squirrel, is endlessly curious, lively and friendly. They're natural acrobats, too!

Chinchillas are a rodent. Like all the rodent pets, they need their own cage for resting and sleeping but want to come out to play for at least 2 hours every day.

Also, like all rodents, they need wood chews to keep their teeth in good condition.

One of the things to love about them is their very thick, velvety fur. Chinchillas have the softest, thickest fur of any animal in the world. It can be white, gray, charcoal, black, tan or violet-blue.

Most rodent pets live for only a few years, but pet chinchillas can live until they're 25 years old. So, if

CHAPTER 7 - CHINCHILLAS

This is a grey chinchilla. Photo by Cameron's Chinchillas.

you choose a chinchilla as your new pet, you're going to have them for a long time!

Here are some very odd things about chinchillas:

- They are almost always born as twins.
- They're born with their eyes already open and with a full coat of fur.
- They're such good jumpers that they can jump 6 feet (almost 2 m). That can easily get them to the top of your refrigerator!

- They have almost no smell.
- They can't sweat. When they get too hot, their ears turn red.
- Getting wet is dangerous for them.
- Their fur is so thick that they don't get fleas.
- They need a daily dust bath to keep clean. You can get pumice dust at pet stores. You'll have fun watching your pet enjoy their bath!

Chinchillas are a mostly quiet pet, but they love attention. Unlike other small pets, they can learn to get along with other pets, like a kitten, guinea pig or small dog.

Chinchillas came from high in the Andes Mountains in the South American countries of Bolivia, Peru, Chile and Argentina. They are used to living in cool places, but with their very thick fur coats they can't be in a room that is warmer than 70 degrees F. (21 degrees C.) For this reason, you'll need air conditioning in the hot months to help them stay healthy.

Getting wet is dangerous for them because if they don't get completely dry right away they can develop skin infections or fur rot. If they accidentally get wet, dry them with a hair dryer on the "cool" setting.

And because they're curious explorers and chewers, like all rodents, when you let them out to race around your house, which they love to do, you need to be sure you've already pet-proofed it. This means no electric cords just waiting to be chewed on, no places they could hide, and no other dangers.

When you pet-proof, ask yourself these questions:

- Are there covers on all the wires and everything made of wood?
- Are windows closed? Or, if open, are the screens secure?
- Is the room the right temperature for them to be comfortable?
- Are books and magazines or anything made of paper put away where they can't get it?
- If there are curtains or blinds on the windows, are they tucked out of the way, with no strings or fabric my pet can chew on or get tangled in?

Generally, if a room would be safe for a child who is two years old to play in, it will be safe for your pet. Of course, you will always be there to supervise any time your pet, or a very young child, is running around in that room.

Chinchillas are a social animal, used to living in groups. You could get just one, but they will be lonely. It's better to have two chinchillas, and best if this can be the twins born together. If that's not possible, get two who are the same age, already know each other and the same gender. Getting the same gender means you get two boys, or two girls.

Chinchillas can be a good first pet for kids who know how to be gentle with animals. They don't like to be picked up and held. Like cats, they'd rather come to you when they want to sit in your lap.

They need a large wire cage with a solid floor, shelves to climb up to, a food dish, water dish and their dust bath dish. The cage should be at least 3 feet long, 2 feet wide and 2 feet high (1m, 70 cm, 70 cm) for one chinchilla and 6 feet long, 6 feet wide and 3 feet high (2 m, 2 m, 1 m) for two chinchillas.

Their cage needs paper bedding thick enough for them to burrow in, and it will need to be spot-cleaned every day. You'll need to do a complete cage cleaning twice a week.

Chinchillas like to have lots of toys. They especially love cardboard boxes to play with. Some also like to have a large exercise wheel with no spokes and a solid floor. Get them some soft toys, wood toys and wood chews and soft pieces of fabric.

Each chinchilla needs their own sleeping box. If you have two chinchillas, also give them another larger sleeping box for when they want to sleep together.

Put their cage away from drafts, including the breeze from your air conditioning. It also needs to be away from direct sunlight, since chinchillas easily overheat.

Wild chinchillas eat grasses, plants and tree bark. Pet chinchillas eat pellets and timothy hay. They also like fresh vegetables. Their favourite treat is raisins.

If your chinchilla starts chewing on their fur, it could be because they're bored, stressed or they aren't getting healthy food.

Chinchillas make soft grunting noises, but they can also chirp, squeal, bark and make a sound like having the hiccups.

Chapter 8

Snakes

Some pets are fun because they're smart and can learn to do tricks.

Some are so fluffy and cute you just want to hug them.

Some are great to play with.

And some are good pets because they are so different than people. It's fascinating to watch them, up close. And imagine what it would be like to be them.

Reptile pets are in the 'really interesting to watch' group of pets. Most reptiles don't want to be pets and never can be a good pet. They'd much rather have their wild life.

But there are some reptiles that can learn to live with people. There are a few lizards and snakes that are bred to be pets. They can be friendly, safe to have and somewhat easy to care for.

If you've never had a pet before, start with an easy pet to have, like a gerbil or a hamster. Once

This is a California kingsnake.

you've gained some pet parenting skills, you'll be ready for a more demanding pet, like a reptile or a dog. You can find out more about good beginner pets in another book in this series, Small Fun Pets; Beginner Pets for Kids 9-12.

Here something to think about if you already have a pet or pets. Sometimes it can seem so exciting to get a new pet that you almost forget about the pet or pets you already have. This isn't kind or fair. It also isn't responsible pet care.

Make sure you have enough time to keep your promises to every pet you get!

CHAPTER 8 - SNAKES

This is a corn snake. Photo by Kapa65 via Pixabay.

Safe and Fun Pet Snakes

There are six types of snakes that can make good pets. They are the Kingsnake, Corn Snake, Milk Snake, Gopher Snake, Rosy Boa and Ball Python.

Ball Pythons have a scary name, but they're popular because they are very docile (say this word like this: DOS-sigh-ill or like this: DOS-ill). Docile means tame and meek.

53

This is good when you want a pet snake you can take out of their tank and hold or show your friends.

Before you get a pet snake, you need to know they eat live food and the food they want to eat is baby mice. Some pet snakes will accept a mouse that has been frozen and then thawed before you give it to them. Others refuse to eat a mouse unless they hunt it and kill it themselves.

How do you feel about having live, or frozen, feeder mice in your home? How do the people you live with, like parents, brothers or sisters or room-mates feel about this? Not everyone is comfortable with the eating habits of reptile pets!

Another thing to know is that all snakes have a strong instinct to explore their territory. Even if they seem very lazy, they are escape artists who can be very clever about getting out of their tanks. They want to have a look around your home. They could get into trouble, like being stuck down a drain.

It can be very hard to find a snake that is lost in your home.

When you adopt a pet snake, you are promising to give it good care for a long time. Pet snakes can live for 20 years, or more. Think carefully about this question: Do you think you will still want this pet for a long time?

If so, you're ready to decide which type of snake you want. Next, you need to buy everything they need as you get ready to choose your new pet. You need their tank set up and running properly before you bring them home.

Here's what a pet snake needs

Snakes need a glass tank with an escape-proof canopy top. If the type of snake you choose is a ground snake, they need a long tank that isn't very high. If they're a tree snake, they need a tall tank that isn't very wide.

Snakes want to feel cozy in their tank, just like wild snakes do in their dens. A tank that is too big will make them feel anxious (except when they want to go look for a better place to sleep or hide).

On the bottom of their tank you need some bedding. This can be clean fine sand, small smooth river stones or reptile bedding. You could also use newspaper, but it doesn't look as good.

Next, give your pet some stones and branches to climb on and hide in. All snakes need a little cave or den to rest and sleep. This could be a bowl or flower pot or a clean cardboard box with one side cut out for a door.

All reptile pets need a basking light. This is so they can warm up when they need to. They also need a branch or flat rock where they can be close enough to their basking light, but not so close they could be hurt.

Some snakes also need an ultraviolet-B (UV-B) lamp unless they can get some natural sunlight every day. You'll also need a heating pad under just part of the tank.

And your tank needs instruments to measure the temperature and humidity. Humidity means how much

This is another type of king snake. Photo by sipa on Pixabay.

moisture there is in the air. Thermometers measure temperature. Hydrometers measure humidity.

Some parts of the tank must be a bit warmer and some a bit cooler, so your pet always has a choice. You need to watch the air temperature, floor temperature and humidity several times every day and a few times through the night to be sure it is ideal before you put your new pet into their new home.

Snakes need a water dish. Some like one that is big enough for them to have a dip. They need extra moisture when they shed their skin.

Generally, snakes are happiest when they live alone. You can have two corn snakes together in one tank, but then you need a bigger tank.

Spot clean the tank and check the humidity and temperatures daily. Take everything out of the tank, clean it and give your pet fresh bedding and a slightly different tank arrangement once a month. Part of the fun of having a snake is thinking up new, interesting tank set-ups that your pet will enjoy exploring and relaxing in.

Reptile shows are a good place to learn more about pet snakes and see lots of healthy animals that are for sale. This is where you can see morphs. Morphs are pets bred to have interesting colours, patterns or other things about them that pet owners want.

Pet snakes aren't the easiest or cheapest pet to get and keep. You could spend a lot of money on a fancy tank and an unusual morph of your favourite type of snake.

If you don't want to spend a lot of money, look for good used tanks and tank equipment in yard sales and the free online ads for your area. There's always someone who wants to sell their snake or reptile pet set-up. It can be possible to get your new pet and everything it needs for less than $100. Then you'll need to buy feeder mice and tank bedding.

If your snake eats frozen mice, you need freezer space to keep them. If your pet refuses to eat frozen mice, you'll need to buy live mice and look after the mice until they become your snake's dinner. When they do, you need to be there. A frightened mouse will fight back and could hurt your snake.

Chapter 9

Cockatiels

Parrots have the reputation of being a difficult pet. This is because they can be loud, they want a lot of attention and they can be very needy pets.

But there is one type of parrot that can be a pleasure to have as a new family member. It's the cockatiel, a small parrot that comes from Australia. Today, all pet cockatiels are captive bred. This means their parents and grandparents and great-grandparent birds were all pets.

If you live in Australia or go there for a visit, you could still see wild cockatiels. Or you might see them at a zoo.

They can be grey, white, chocolate brown, tan, silver, green or yellow. All cockatiels have a long tail, a plume crest on their heads and rosy cheeks.

All cockatiels are acrobats and clowns, eager to entertain you. They love playing games and can learn to do tricks, like Step Up! when you want them to climb onto your fingers. One of the things they really like to do, that some kids think is just hilarious, is

CHAPTER 9 - COCKATIELS

This cockatiel is likely male because of the large number of yellow and orange feathers he has.

take a shower with you! They also like watching TV with the family.

If you choose a cockatiel as your pet, you should know that this is a pet that can live for a long time, as long as 20 years.

You'll probably want a male, because the males are the ones that have brighter colours, and are better at whistling, singing songs, dancing to tunes and learning words. Most of the young cockatiels you see at pet stores are females, who make good pets but, because they usually aren't as good as the males at whistling and other tricks, female cockatiels usually cost less than males.

Here's a fun thing female cockatiels do. They're brilliant at mimicking sounds! Mimic means hearing a sound and being able to make that sound. When female cockatiels hear an interesting sound, like a phone ringing, someone grunting or the toilet flushing, they might start making that sound all the time!

Sometimes this will be hilarious. But it could get annoying if they just won't stop. Give your cockatiel lots of different sounds to enjoy so she'll stop repeating the same ones over and over!

All cockatiels are fascinated by sounds! They learn to recognize the people they care about by the sounds they make, like the sounds of you getting home every day.

To see lots of different cockatiels and meet their breeders, go to a Bird Show. These are held in big cities once or twice a year. It's a great place to find the perfect parrot for you!

Cockatiels are friendly, gentle, easy to tame and they like to be held and petted. If you have just one, they are more likely to whistle or try to talk, but they also will want to spend more time hanging out with you. One of the things they love to do is sit on your shoulder, while you're reading or watching TV.

If you get two cockatiels, they'll keep each other company and will be content with only one or two hours a day of playing outside their cage or hanging out with you. But when you have two cockatiels, they'll also be less likely to want to talk or whistle.

Some owners feed their cockatiels with parrot pellets, but they're healthier when they eat a mix of cockatiel seeds and some fresh fruit and vegetables, a bit of cooked meat and a hard-boiled egg every day. There are many types of parrots that can be pets, so

CHAPTER 9 - COCKATIELS

This exotic cockatiel lives in a zoo. Photo by LenaSevcikova on Pixabay.

be sure to get the seed mix that is especially for cockatiels.

Like people, cockatiels sleep at night and are active during the day. They want to wake up slowly, as it gets light out. They feel sleepy just after the sun sets, just like most people.

Also like people, parrots are individuals. Some are a little more shy than others. Getting to know your new pet's personality is part of the fun of having a pet!

A cockatiel that wants to be petted will lower its head or gently nibble your fingers. They also like having their head and neck scratched and taking treats from your hand.

If your cockatiel is hissing, they're not pleased about something. To be sure you're getting the message, they may tap their beak on a solid surface, like the side of their cage.

Cockatiels are a pet that wants to know their family members are near-by. They love to chew on anything made of paper, so when they're out of their cage, you'll need to protect your books or magazines.

Cockatiels are one of the types of pets that like to see themselves in a mirror. But cockatiels think it's another bird they're seeing, so having a mirror could also make them anxious when the 'other' bird isn't friendly. You could try giving your cockatiel a mirror, just to see if they like it or not.

They are a messy bird, tossing their food around and losing feathers, so you will need to change their cage bedding, food and water and clean their cage every day.

Cockatiels want a large cage to climb around and explore, so get the largest one you can. A cage meant for a parakeet or budgie, canary or finch isn't nearly big enough for a cockatiel or a pair of cockatiels. It should be a metal cage, with a wide door and the type of food and water containers that don't spill. This will make cage cleaning easier.

Choose a cockatiel that's been hand- raised because they've already learned to be a good pet and

This is another type of cockatiel that has mostly yellow or white feathers. Photo by Albina01 on Pixabay.

trust people. Young cockatiels who've only known their parents or flocks are semi-wild and may never become a contented pet, making you and them unhappy.

A fun fact about cockatiels is that both the males and females are good parents! They are the only type of parrot that look after their eggs and raise their babies together. Males usually sit on the eggs at night, and females during the day.

Chapter 10
Kittens or Cats

Kittens are a lot of fun! They race around, play-fighting with their brothers and sisters, getting into all sorts of mischief. They seem to have endless energy, never staying still for a moment until they fall into a furry heap for another nap!

They quickly grow into cats that seem to be perfectly happy to be left on their own, just as long as their food dish is always full and their litter box is always clean.

Cats can be just as friendly and loving as dogs can be. It's just that dogs are eager to please people. Cats aren't.

Dogs love learning tricks and showing off what they know. Cats couldn't care less. They might learn to come when you call them and a few tricks, but they'll only do them when they feel like it.

You can play with dogs outside. Cats are better off inside. They'd rather cuddle than run around. Cats can be a totally indoor pet and be healthy and happy. This

CHAPTER 10 – KITTENS OR CATS

This is an adult orange tabby cat. Photo by Alexas Fotos on Pixabay.

isn't true for dogs, who need to get outside at least twice a day.

Cats are meat eaters. They can't have dog food, which has meat, grains and vegetables. Kittens and cats that are ill need soft cat food, but healthy adult cats eat dry cat food.

Cats are snackers. They like to have a few bites of food several times a day. It might seem like they don't like to drink water, but they need fresh water daily, as all living creatures do.

Don't give your adult cat milk to drink. Many cats get stomach aches when they have cow milk or goat milk. They're lactose intolerant, just like some people are.

This is a young kitten. Photo by StockSnap via Pixabay.

You can buy cat treats or use little bits of cooked liver, fish or chicken as a treat for your cat.

Here are the tasks you'll need to do to keep them healthy:

- Give them a pan of litter. Spot clean it every few days and completely replace the litter every few weeks. Never use the kind of litter that clumps with kittens. It can kill them if they accidentally swallow it. Cats can be very fussy about their litter, and won't like it if you change types all the time. If you don't clean it as often as your cat wants, they will protest by peeing and pooping on the floor.
- Gently clean their ears with a moist cloth or a cotton ball.

- Clip their nails. You only need to do this a few times a year.
- Brush their coat, once or twice a day for a long-haired cat and once or twice a week for a short-haired cat.
- Take them to the vet. All kittens need their shots to protect them from serious diseases. They also need to be checked for worms; many kittens have them. Most shelter kittens and cats have already had their first shots and been checked for worms.
- Cats need to be neutered (a minor operation that will mean they can't have kittens) to help them be healthier. This also stops males from spraying their pee to mark their territory. If your cat has watery eyes or is sneezing, they probably have a cold and need to see the vet.

Something you won't have to do is teach your cat how to use her litter box. Kittens usually learn how to do this from their mother. When they have left their mother too soon, you can gently put a kitten in the litter box right after she eats. Cats are very good at getting the idea right away!

This is another thing that makes them a bit easier pet to have than a dog.

Kittens can grow up to be as affectionate or independent as you want them to be. If you want a loving cat, you need to handle them a lot, letting them sit on your lap or playing with them on the floor. Kittens think everything is a toy. They just love having a cardboard box as a playhouse with some doors and windows cut into it. They're also fascinated by paper bags and will hop into an open school bag or suitcase.

They also like warm, cozy places to hide.

Though cats can't learn all the tricks dogs can, they can learn to come when you call them, take a treat from your hand, fetch a toy and walk on a leash.

Get them a scratching post so they won't scratch the furniture or shred the cushions and chairs. Cats that don't get outside to hunt are more likely to be chewers of slippers or cushions. Give them a toy made with real sheepskin or rabbit fur. They'll switch to chewing the toy instead.

Cats also like to chew on houseplants. Instead, give them some cat grass. Buy the seeds and plant them, like you would plant a Bunny garden (see Chapter 6 for how to this). Your cat will chew some grass whenever it has a stomach ache.

Indoor cats can live for a long time. Getting to age 13 is average, but some cats live into their 20s!

Chapter 11
Puppies or Dogs

Of all the pets in this book, dogs are the most like people in the ways they think and behave. They are also the most like people in what they like to eat, what they enjoy doing and in what they need to stay healthy and happy.

Pet dogs don't want to just live with you and get together to play sometimes. They want to do everything you're doing, all the time. Other pets can be left alone sometimes and maybe even be on their own for a day or two, but not dogs. They're a pack animal, meaning they live in family groups with one leader, the Alpha dog.

Not only are they miserable when their family leaves them alone, they truly don't know what to do. This is when 'bad' dog behaviour, like peeing on the carpet or destroying the living room, happens. They don't mean to misbehave. They're just terribly anxious and afraid.

Dogs do best when they get lots of time and attention from their Alpha dog (that's their owner) and their family. If you homeschool or there is someone in

A mother golden retriever and her pup. Photo by Jaclou via Pixabay.

your family at home almost all the time, you could have a happy dog as a pet.

But if you're at school all day and other people in your family are also away at school or work, your dog will be worried and angry or afraid. Having two dogs helps, but that might not be enough to keep your dog content while she waits for you to come home.

Dogs need to go outside several times a day to pee and poop and need one or two walks every day for exercise. And all dogs need to go to puppy school to learn dog manners like how to walk on their leash without pulling and not jumping up.

Housetraining is something cats learn by themselves, but dogs find harder to understand. They

CHAPTER 11 – PUPPIES OR DOGS

Dogs love car rides. Photo by Herney via Pixabay.

know not to pee in their bed, but might think everywhere else is the same as being outside. You'll need to be very patient with your puppy while they learn all their lessons about how to be a good dog as well as a good pet and a pleasant member of your family.

There's a lot of variety among dogs – types, sizes and what they look like. Bigger dogs tend to be more patient with other pets and children, but they also eat more so they cost more to have. Smaller breeds of dogs are better if you have a small home or live in a flat or condo. But small dogs are usually the noisier breeds.

Dogs can live for a long time, as long as 15 years with proper care.

For all these reasons, dogs are the most difficult pet to have of all the pets in this book. They can be

A puppy playing with a rope toy. Photo by Pixels courtesy of Pixabay.

wonderful friends, loving and loyal, but before you get a dog you need to know that caring for them is a big responsibility. Dogs aren't a good choice as your very first pet.

Here's how to pick a puppy:

- He or she should be alert, plump, smell good and have shiny eyes and thick fur.
- If the ears smell, he has an ear infection.
- A puppy that has a dull coat, runny eyes, a cough, or is skinny has been neglected. They probably won't make a good pet because, to be a pet, an animal needs kind and gentle handling from the time they are very young.
- Don't pick the puppy that whimpers, is shy, doesn't want to explore or doesn't want to come over to see you.

CHAPTER 11 – PUPPIES OR DOGS

- You don't want the pup that yaps, growls or whines a lot. They'll grow up still doing this all the time.
- Don't pick a puppy because you feel sorry for it. It might be sickly, fearful or aggressive when it grows up, even with a lot of loving care and attention from you. Always pick the most confident, healthy, happy puppy.

Here's what you need when you bring your puppy home. A dog bed in a quiet corner, a halter-style leash, bowls for food and water that can't tip over, newspapers for housetraining and dog food. You'll also need chew toys, soft toys, nail trimmers and a brush.

Some dogs hardly ever need a bath but puppies, white dogs and dogs with oily or woolly coats need regular baths in warm water. Use dog shampoo. Shampoo meant for people will give them skin rashes.

Remember that puppies have new teeth and they need to use them. They try to chew everything, including plastic toys, electric and computer cords, your socks or anything they can steal from the laundry basket, medicines that aren't put away, bones they find in the garbage pail, and anything else they can get at. It's up to you to protect them from danger.

Shouting at your pet when they do something wrong doesn't make any sense to them. Instead, do what you'd do with a child who is very young, say 18 months old. Say "No" in a growly voice, then smile and offer them a toy or just change their attention to something better.

This happy dog is a mixed breed. Photo by SmBerG on Pixabay.

There's a lot more to learn about having a dog and being a good dog pet parent. This is much more than you need to learn to give good care to pets that are easier to have, like a gerbil or chinchilla. If you decide that a dog is the best pet for you, but your parents say they don't think so, you might need to prove to them that you are ready to be a responsible dog owner.

Do this by learning all you can about dogs and other pets and how to give good pet care.

Offer to dog-walk and dog-sit for family members or neighbours so you get to know what it's like to care for a dog.

Think about everything a dog needs.

- Will you always remember to feed your dog, give it fresh water and not complain about having to clean up when they make a mess?
- Who will walk your dog every day? Will you want to do this, even when it's raining or cold out?
- Do you have the time to go to puppy and dog obedience classes with your pet and practice what you learn there at home?
- How will you pay for getting your dog and buying it everything they need? This includes their food, toys, puppy school classes and visits to the vet.
- Dogs can live a long time. Are you sure you'll want this dog for 10 years, or more?

One of the fun things about having a dog is they like to be with you, doing what you're doing.

They'll be overjoyed if that's playing games, running in the park or on the beach, going for a swim or a car ride.

Dogs can learn more tricks than any other type of pet. Some tricks you might want to teach your dog are how to fetch a toy or a stick, sit up and beg, roll over or dance with you. Dogs can learn the meanings of a lot of words, too, including the names of everyone in their pack. Their pack is your family.

Of all the animals in this book, dogs are the most expensive to get, the most work to keep, but they might just be the top fun pet for kids, or anyone who has a place in their home and their heart for a new best friend!

Chapter 12

How to Bring Your New Pet Home

Here's how to get ready to bring your new pet home.

Begin by getting everything they'll need:

- A cage or tank and the right type of cage bedding for the type of pet they are, if you're getting a rodent pet.
- A pet bed if you're getting a cat or dog.
- Food and water dishes or bottles that won't spill.
- Nail trimmers and a brush.
- Wood chews for rodent pets or chew toys for dogs or cat treats for your kitten or cat
- Other toys
- A pet-carrier, for travelling in the car or a car pet harness for a dog.
- The right type of food for your new pet
- Pet-safe cleaning supplies and old towels for cleaning

It's important to get your home, and their future home, set up first before you buy your new pet.

CHAPTER 12 – HOW TO BRING YOUR NEW PET HOME

A group of kittens playing in a basket. Photo by Noly courtesy of Pixabay.

Think about how scary it is for them to leave the home they have now, where they feel safe and always get water and food. They're coming to a new place that looks strange, smells strange and has strange new people to get used to. Of course they're nervous and afraid at first!

Be kind and be patient. Don't try to pick them up and pet them right away. Instead, let them settle in and get used to the new smells and sounds of their home. Soon, they'll notice that you bring them food. When they come close, you can gently touch them, but don't try to grab them. They might think you are attacking them and try to fight back!

Soon, they will begin to trust you and want to know you better. You need to take it slow, just like you do when making new people friends.

It's best to get a pet that is old enough to leave his mother, but not an adult yet. They're going to adjust to their new life in your family faster than an adult pet would.

Where to find your new pet

A great place to look for your new pet is at a rescue shelter. They have animals that have been checked out by a vet, have had their shots, are healthy and are ready to find their new home.

A good place to find your new pet is at a pet show. You can meet the breeders and ask questions about this pet!

A bad place to find your new pet is ordering them online to be shipped to you. Being closed up in a box and sent somewhere is very stressful for an animal. They could arrive very upset, dehydrated or very sick.

How to pick up a small pet

Imagine what it would be like if you were a little pet. All humans, even kids, would look like huge monsters, wouldn't they?

Until you got to know them, they'd be terrifying. You'd be so afraid they might grab you and crush you. Or drop you. Or even eat you!

If you want your pet to see you as a friend, not a monster enemy, one thing you need to do is learn how to pick them up so no one gets hurt.

CHAPTER 12 – HOW TO BRING YOUR NEW PET HOME

This is a very young rabbit. Photo by Taboadahdez courtesy of Pixabay.

You do this by scooping them up and holding them under their belly and bum with one hand, and with a hand gently holding the top of their body with your

Be very gentle when picking up young animals. They can be very easily hurt.

other hand. Never lift any creature by a foot, leg, tail or the back of their neck.

If you have other pets, be slow and careful introducing them to your new pet. Sometimes, dogs or cats see rodent pets as prey. Prey means another animal they hunt and kill. A prey pet like a guinea pig or mouse will be very frightened of a cat. You can't teach your cat not to try to pounce on your smaller pets. It's their instinct to behave this way. It's better to be sure all your pets are protected from any dangers in your home.

Give your new pet all the time they need to settle in their new home and family. Don't invite lots of people to meet your pet right away.

Don't shout at your pet, talk very loudly near their ears, scream or hit them. They won't understand, they'll just be very frightened. They'll learn to fear you, and they might be so scared that they bite.

Poison Foods for Pets

These are poisonous for many pets:

- Raw potatoes
- Onions or garlic
- Chocolate
- Anything that has caffeine in it, like coffee, tea or soda pop
- Avocados
- Some house plants, including poinsettias
- Cow milk or goat milk or anything with lactose in it
- Anything with alcohol in it
- Some medicines made for people

Now you know how to keep your pet healthy, safe and happy, it's time to decide...

Chapter 13
What Pet Will You Get?

So, what is the best pet for you?

If you want a **quiet pet**, choose a snake, hamster, gerbil, rat or cat.

If you want an **active pet**, choose a gerbil, chinchilla, kitten or dog.

If you want a **pet that mostly lives in their tank or cage**, choose a snake, gerbil or hamster.

If you want a **furry pet**, choose a rabbit, cavy, chinchilla, cat or dog.

If you want a **pet that's fun to play with**, choose a gerbil, rat, cavy, chinchilla, rabbit or dog.

If you want a **pet that likes to hang out with you**, choose a gerbil, guinea pig, rat, rabbit, cat or dog.

If you want a **pet that understands words**, choose a cat or dog.

If you want an **unusual pet**, choose a snake, chinchilla or one of the special breeds of cats or dogs.

CHAPTER 15 - WHAT PET WILL YOU GET?

A pet rabbit playing in a sandbox. Photo by Pezibear courtesy of Pixabay.

If you want a **pet that can learn tricks**, choose a tuxedo (black and white) cat or a dog.

If you're **allergic to pets**, choose a hairless cat or a snake.

If you need a pet that is **OK on its own for a few days** (like over the weekend in your classroom, or if you go away for two or three days), choose a pet rodent such as a cavy, rat, hamster or gerbil. Or, with enough food and water out and an extra litter box, a cat can be left alone and be perfectly content on its own for a few days.

Animal Group Names

In English, we have a name for when you have two or more of an animal. These names are called Collective Nouns.

The collective noun for more than one person is group of people or crowd of people.

Sometimes, the collective nouns for animals can be amusing. You might laugh when you hear some of the collective nouns for the pets you've read about in this book! These are:

- A horde of hamsters
- A business of gerbils
- A drift of guinea pigs
- A mischief of rats
- A herd of rabbits
- A colony of chinchillas
- A den of snakes
- A company of cockatiels
- A clowder of cats
- A pack of dog

THANK YOU FOR READING!

THANK YOU for reading!

I I hope you've enjoyed meeting the interesting and fun pets in this book.

Do you know which one you want yet?

Once you choose your new pet, you'll want to learn LOTS more about them. To do this, you could go to pet shows, read about pets online, or read more pet books. There are so many interesting things to learn about pets, I know you'll have as much fun finding out more about them as having them!

Wishing you many happy times

Jacquelyn

About Jacquelyn

Jacquelyn Elnor Johnson writes books about pets for children. Her family has just one pet, a cat named Boots. But in the past, there have been many wonderful dogs in her life, including Dachshunds, Poodles and a black Labrador Retriever.

She and her family live in Nova Scotia, Canada.

THANK YOU FOR READING!

More fun pet and animal books you might like, all written for kids who are 9 to 12, or in grades three to seven:

Best Pets for Kids Series:

    I Want a Puppy, or a Dog

    I Want a Kitten, or a Cat

    I Want a Bearded Dragon

    I Want a Leopard Gecko

Fun Pets for Kids Series:

    Small Fun Pets; Beginner Pets for Kids 9-12

    Top 10 Fun Pets for Kids 9-12

Fun Animal Facts for Kids Series:

    Fun Dog Facts for Kids 9-12

    Fun Cat Facts for Kids 9-12

    Fun Leopard Gecko and Bearded Dragon Facts for Kids 9-12

    Fun Reptile Facts for Kids 9-12; Lizards, Turtles, Crocodilians, Snakes and Birds

Investigate more books for curious kids right here:

www.BestPetsForKids.fun

www.ingramcontent.com/pod-product-compliance
Lightning Source LLC
Chambersburg PA
CBHW061745290426
43673CB00095B/270